PRAYERS for *Everyday Living*

Presented to:

_____

Given By:

_____

Date:

_____

PRAYERS for *Everyday Living*

KEITH GWALTNEY

VM

Copyright © 2023 Keith Gwaltney

No part of this publication may be reproduced, stored in a retrieval system, or transmitted in any form or by any means, electronic, mechanical, photocopying, recording, scanning, or otherwise, without the prior written permission of the author.

ISBN: 979-8-9856215-3-2 (Paperback)
ISBN: 979-8-9856215-2-5 (E-Book)

Front Cover Design by: Olivia Pro Design

Published by: Visual Ministries, Fleming Island, FL. United States
First printing 2023

www.keithgwaltney.com

Contents

Introduction	1
Anger	2
Anxiety	3
Authority	4
Belief	5
Blessings	6
Children	7
Church	8
Compassion	9
Condemned	10
Confidence	11
Contentment	12
Courage/Fear	13
Decisions/Discernment	14
Deliverer	15

Depression	16
Discipleship	17
Discouraged	18
Encouragement	19
Eternal Life	20
Faith	21
Fellowship	22
Finances	23
Forgiveness	24
Freedom	25
Future	26
Giving	27
Goals	28
Grace	29
Grief	30
Guidance	31
Healing/Sickness	32
Heaven	33
Holiness	34
Hope	35

Identity	36
Joy	37
Life	38
Lonely	39
Love	40
Marriage	41
Meditation	42
Mercy	43
Obedience	44
Patience	45
Peace	46
Praise	47
Prayer	48
Protection	49
Purpose	50
Rebellions	51
Redemption	52
Repentance	53
Rest	54
Righteousness	55

Salvation	56
Satan	57
Scripture	58
Security	59
Self-Worth	60
Serving	61
Singleness	62
Stability	63
Stewardship	64
Strength	65
Temptation	66
Thankfulness	67
Thoughts	68
Trouble	69
Trust	70
Truth	71
Unsaved	72
Victory	73
Wisdom	74
Witnessing	75

Work	76
Worried	77
About the author	78

Introduction

"Prayers for Everyday Living" has been created to provide a prayer for the 76 topics covered in my first book "Scriptures for Everyday Living." As I continue to grow in my relationship with the Lord, I desire to continue to share with others what God teaches me. For our relationship with God to grow, we must be willing to spend time with Him. There are two main parts to achieving this. One, hearing from Him by being in His Word, and two, talking with Him through prayer. The prayers in this book are to help get you started when facing one of the 76 topics listed. God loves to hear from His children. Through prayer, it is just you having a conversation with The Father.

Anger

Father, I pray that I become a person who is quick to listen, slow to speak, and slow to get angry. Help me surrender myself to Your Word, becoming humble and possessing a gentle and quiet spirit. I know the worst emotion I can bring to any situation is anger. I know that I cannot do it without You. Help to open my ears and my heart to what it is that You want to teach me during these difficult situations. Lord, help me not desire revenge when done wrong but to know that it is Yours to avenge. Give me a heart that forgives and eyes to see that others need forgiveness just like I do. Help me to grow and exercise self-control. Father, help me to bring calmness and not rage. In Jesus' name, I pray, Amen.

Anxiety

Father, I come to You filled with anxiety, worry, and fear. The what ifs? are taking charge of my thinking. Fill me now with Your Spirit and give me the peace that passes all understanding. Help me to live by faith, knowing that You have given me the authority over any thoughts or plans of the enemy. I bind this feeling of anxiety now in Jesus' name. I turn from the stress of this world and the racing thoughts in my mind to sit at Your feet and rest in Your love and comfort. Thank You, Father, for You are still in control. Thank You for Your faithfulness, unconditional love, and never changing ways. In Jesus' name, Amen.

Authority

Father, we know that today, You have a kingdom purpose. Nothing that is happening in this world is a surprise to You. You see the big picture and are at work in ways that we cannot see. Father, I thank You that based on Your Word, You have given the believer, the born-again child of God, power and authority over the enemy and his works here on earth. Thank You that the One in me is greater than anyone in this world. Father, help me to understand the power I have within my words. Purify me with Your Holiness, that I may be a worthy vessel that communicates Your power and glory to this generation. In Jesus' name, Amen.

Belief

Father, even the disciples who walked with Jesus needed to strengthen their faith. Jesus told them that they could uproot trees and crumble mountains if their faith was only the size of a mustard seed. Lord, I need more faith like the disciples. Increase my faith and make me a mover of mountains. Grow my belief in You alone so that I would be strong in the Lord and ready to battle against the doubts planted by the enemy. You know what I need, and You provide for all my cares. Father, increase my faith! In Jesus' name, Amen.

Blessings

Thank You, Father, for declaring us righteous through Jesus Christ. Thank You for surrounding us with favor as a shield. We ask that we walk in Your blessing and goodness today. May Your face shine on us. Open the right doors for our lives and loved ones. Close the wrong doors to protect us from those we need to walk away from.

May the favor of the Lord our God rest on us; establish the work of our hands and bring to fulfillment all that You have given us to do this day. Give us a heart of wisdom to hear Your voice. Keep us strong with Your favor and grace. In Jesus' name, Amen.

Children

Dear Father, being blessed with another day, I want to release my children straight into Your tender care. I know that is the best place they could ever be. Thank You in advance for everything You have in store for this day, this season, and their lives. I ask for Your wisdom and direction over their day. Give them understanding beyond their years and teach them Your ways. Protect them from feelings of shame or condemnation and cover them with Your grace and hope. I pray that You surround them with friends and leaders who will challenge them to press closer to You. May they know who they are in Christ and live a life that is pleasing to You. In Jesus' name, Amen.

Church

Father, I pray for our pastor and the priorities of the congregation. Thank You for our pastor and his heart to serve You. Teach him Your ways so that he knows You and finds favor with You as he leads us. Give us ears to hear what Your Spirit is saying to our church and open our eyes to see things as You see them. Lord, strengthen our love for one another as a body. May our love for others show that we are Your disciples. Give us a spirit of one so that we may glorify You with one heart and voice. Bring us to a place where our words "Your kingdom come, Your will be done on earth as it is in heaven" are more than words being said. It is in Jesus' name I pray, Amen.

Compassion

Father, I ask that You remove any hate or bitterness from my heart and replace that with Your mercy and compassion. I pray that You would have compassion for my doubts, fears, actions, thoughts, and the wrestling that happens in me. Show me new ways, Lord. Help me extend that compassion not only to myself but to others. Help me to take the love that You give and share that with those that I come in contact with. Father, thank You for this time of prayer and all the compassion You give freely to Your children. I love You and give thanks in Jesus' name, Amen.

Condemned

Thank You, Father, for Your son Jesus Christ, who has already endured condemnation for my sake. Thanks to Your love for me, I no longer am condemned for the sins I committed knowingly or unknowingly. Therefore, I will not live in pain, hurt, or shame my past has caused me, but I will focus on Christ, who sets me free from all bondage. Through Christ, I declare that I am a victor and not a victim of condemnation. I will not feel condemned but continue to live in my salvation, victory, strength, and freedom. Thank You, Jesus Christ, for enduring the cross of Calvary for my condemnation. Thank You, Father, for sending Your son to save anyone who will believe. In Jesus' name, Amen.

Confidence

Heavenly Father, oh, how good You are. You give me strength when my heart and mind are weak. You encourage me even during times of doubt. Thank You that even when I struggle to remember that I am a child of the most high, You are still right here with me wherever I go. You made plans for me, for my good, to prosper, protect, and most importantly, share Your love. I commit my ways and my life to You! I Know If You are in the middle of the plans, then they can have success in the ways that You see success! I can do all things through You, Father! Help me now to walk in Your ways, full of confidence, knowing that You are with me. In Jesus' name, Amen.

Contentment

Father, so many of us live in a state of discontent when the desire for things consumes our thoughts and actions. We enjoy material things and their day-to-day function in our lives. I pray that You would help me not to be so preoccupied with seeking the things the world offers, for I know it does not satisfy. I thank You, Lord, for the good things You offer from Your abundance, for this is what satisfies my soul. I thank You that I can be content no matter what season of life I am in, whether in need or having more than enough, for my contentment is in You. Thank You for being my provider and knowing what I need. In Jesus' name, Amen.

Courage/Fear

Almighty Father, You strengthen the weak and uphold those who might fall. Therefore, I ask that You give me courage now, for those who trust in You do not need to fear. Give me the help that You have promised to those who ask it, that I may overcome my fears and go bravely forward.

God, help me be strong and courageous without any self-doubt. I pray that the Holy Spirit keeps me walking in truth, knowing who I am in Christ. Do not let me get caught up listening to what others say about me, but may I rely on who You say I am. When tempted to give up, help me keep going forward with the courage to do whatever You call me to do. In Jesus' name, Amen.

Decisions/Discernment

Father, as I make decisions, help me be humble and seek Your face continually. Protect me from my selfish motives. May You give me a spirit of humility and graciousness. Help me to follow Jesus's example on the cross when he said, "Not my will, but thy will be done." I don't want things to be about me. I want them to be about You and Your plans and purposes for my life.

1 Peter 5:6 reads, "Humble yourselves, therefore, under God's mighty hand, that He may lift you up in due time." I'm seeking to humble myself and be open to hearing from You. I want to do what pleases You. Give me discernment and guide my ways. In Jesus' name, Amen.

Deliverer

Heavenly Father, I ask for Your forgiveness and cleansing through the blood of Your Son, the Lord Jesus Christ. Lord Jesus, I now take the authority You have given me, and I command all demonic spirits and all addictions to come out in the name of Jesus. No demonic spirit is welcome in this Holy Temple! I command all curses off my family. Jesus Christ is the way, the truth, and the life. All my sins have been remitted, and I am free from the curse that came because of disobedience and rebellion against the Word of God. Thank You, Heavenly Father; thank You, Lord Jesus; thank You, Holy Spirit, for forgiving and loving me. In Jesus's name, Amen.

Depression

Father, thank You for the grace that You have provided. I pray You will use this difficult time to cause me to go deeper in my relationship with You and that You will get the glory for anything produced in me. Thank You that this weakness does not define me. Since I am Your child, I am represented by what You accomplished on the cross. Help me focus on the truth, which is Your Word, and not how I feel. This depression reveals how dependent I am upon You. I need You to sustain my body and mind and give me good health. I lift this prayer for depression, knowing that You still heal today and are eager to answer my prayer. In Jesus' name, Amen.

Discipleship

Father of love, remove the scales from my eyes and lift the indifference from my heart so that I may see Your vision. Transform my life so that I may accomplish Your purpose. Anoint me with Your spirit that I might bring good news to the oppressed, bind up the brokenhearted, and proclaim release to the captive. Surround me with Your love, fill me with Your grace, and strengthen me for Your service. Empower me to respond to the call of Jesus, deny myself, take up my cross, and follow. Send me to proclaim the good news, and may You receive all the glory. In Jesus' name, I pray, Amen.

Discouraged

Father God, I come casting all my cares, concerns, and troubles upon You. You are my rock in uncertainty, my hope in discouragement. This uncertainty will not last, and I trust that You are sure of what the future holds for me. I know that there is hope, unspeakable joy, unfailing love, sufficient grace, and endless mercy in You. According to Your Word in Matthew 11:28, You said, "Come to me, all you who are weary and burdened, and I will give you rest." I come to You now, Father, trusting and believing in Your Word. You are my comfort and hope. You are the God who knows the beginning from the end, and I place my faith in You to see me through this discouraging time. In Jesus' name, I pray, Amen.

Encouragement

Father, there are days when the reality of our broken world can make it seem like we are alone. Today, I ask that Your light of encouragement would dawn on my friends, family, and myself. As I reflect on who You are, I praise You for being the same yesterday, today, and forever. Let the truth of Your character wash over us and lift our spirits. I ask for Your perfect love to quiet our hearts and Your courage to well up in us. You've promised that You will never leave or forsake us. Nothing is too complicated for You; we know Your Spirit is alive and at work in us. So, I stand on Your promises and lean on Your firm name. I love You and thank You for encouraging me. In Jesus' name, Amen.

Eternal Life

Gracious and loving Heavenly Father, I pray to You, knowing that my sin makes me unworthy. I deserve death because of my sin, but You offer forgiveness. I ask You to forgive me and to fill me with the Holy Spirit. I believe that Jesus is the Son of God and that He died and was resurrected from the dead. I accept the gift of eternal life through Christ Jesus, who was sacrificed for my sin. Help me now in my walk to live by Faith in all You have done and promised me. Thank You for the sacrifice of Jesus and Your unconditional love for me. In Jesus' name, Amen.

Faith

Dear Father, You alone are my refuge and strength. You are my help in times of trouble. I will not fear; instead, I will place my faith and hope in You and Your promises. You are for me! I am Your child, and You love me. You have plans and a purpose for my life. You won't leave me stranded, but You will speak peace during the chaos. You are faithful! As I start my day, I come to You with an open heart and mind, ready to receive Your love and guidance. I pray that You will strengthen my faith and trust in You, even when I face challenges and uncertainty. Guide my ways today as I put my trust in You. In Jesus' name, Amen.

Fellowship

Father God, I pray for my brothers and sisters in Christ. Please help me to be an encouragement to them and help us all to walk in the light together. May we strengthen one another, for it is written that iron sharpens iron. Give us wisdom and bless our time of fellowship together. Thank You for those that You have brought into my life that love You. When two or three gather in Your name, You are there with them. Thank You for those that You have placed in my life that have helped me to grow and learn. Please help me share in that fellowship with others to grow together as believers. In Jesus' name, I pray, Amen.

Finances

Heavenly Father, I surrender my financial affairs and concerns about money to Your divine care and love. I ask that You remove my worries, anxieties, and fears about money and replace them with faith. When I need a financial breakthrough in my life, help me to put You first. Give me the right mindset to accomplish this and see the fruits of Your blessings added to my life. During any season of abundance, may I always remember Proverbs 3:9 to honor You with my wealth, with the first fruits. It is not mine; You have allowed me to have what I have. Thank You for being a provider. In Jesus' name, Amen.

Forgiveness

Father, I know that sin separates me from You. I want to turn away from my sinful past and toward You. I ask that You forgive me of any sin I have committed, knowingly and unknowingly. I pray that You guide my ways moving forward. I believe Jesus Christ died for my sins, was resurrected from the dead, is alive, and hears my prayer. I thank You for The Holy Spirit that lives in me. To help show me right from wrong and to help guide my path in a life that allows me to have a relationship with You. Forgive me now, Father, as I forgive those who have done wrong against me. In Jesus' name, I pray, Amen.

Freedom

Father, thank You that with the Spirit of life in Christ Jesus, we are free from the law of sin and death. May my thoughts and attitude be renewed through Christ Jesus, which displays my new nature.

2 Corinthians 3:17 reads, now the Lord is the Spirit, and where the Spirit of the Lord is, there is freedom. I believe I am a child of God, created in His image, and the devil has no place in my life or power over me. Therefore, Father, may our hearts trust You and Your word entirely. Lord, heal every emotional and psychological wound and restore our self-confidence and self-worth. I believe what the Bible says, "that I am called a child of God," and I claim it over my life. I claim my freedom and accept it in Jesus' name, Amen.

Future

Loving Father, each day as I step further into my future, give me the courage, direction, and patience I need. Remind me that You always journey with me and will never lead me into anything that You won't get me through. I don't know what the future holds, but I know You hold the future. So, bring me to a better tomorrow. Make the days of my life and the life in my days overflow with love, kindness, gratitude, and appreciation. Guide my steps, one at a time, for I want the direction of my future to be the direction You have for me.

Thank You for the gift of my life. May the way I live be my gift back to You, with Your love and guidance. In Jesus' name, I pray, Amen.

Giving

Father, I thank You for all that You have given me. My life is full of an overflow of blessings from You. Thank You for always providing. Lord, I pray that You would develop a giving heart that glorifies You in me and a cheerful heart that desires to give back to You my first fruits. May You give me the wisdom to know what to give, when, and whom to give to. Lord, I know that all good things come from You; this is why my heart fills with thanks and praise. Guide my given now so that it glorifies You and Your kingdom. I ask this in Jesus' name, Amen.

Goals

Father, in life, we learn to set goals. I pray that You will help me to run my race, achieving something that will last forever. Salvation is a gift, but hearing You say, "Well done, good and faithful servant," is worth more than anything I can achieve here on earth. Father, help me to run the race in front of me and to focus on my race and my race alone. It does not matter what the people around me are doing. What matters is what You want to do through me. Father, give me strength when I feel weak and encourage me when I think I am not enough. Most importantly, guide me with the Holy Spirit so that my goals are from You. In Jesus' name, I pray, Amen.

Grace

Gracious Father, I come before You in humility, asking for Your grace and mercy. For You know the temptations of this world. You know my flesh is weak. Father, thank You for 1 Corinthians 10:13, which reminds me that You will not allow temptation beyond what I can bear. That when tempted, You will provide a way out. I need Your help daily to stay strong in my walk with You. Forgive me now of any sins I have committed, knowing and unknowingly. Thank You for Your grace and mercy, Father. Thank You for Your unconditional love. I come to You with thanks and praise. In Jesus' name, Amen.

Grief

Loving Father, the loss of one dear to our hearts can make facing another day difficult. The tears are many, for death is a devastating reality of this life. Yet through the cross, in the death and resurrection of Christ, death has been defeated. Thank You for your promise that one day, You will wipe away every tear from our eyes. There will be no mourning, crying, or pain, for all these things will pass away in Your life-giving presence.

Today, Father, help comfort me in this time of mourning with the presence of Your Holy Spirit and the promises of Your Word. In Jesus' name, I pray, Amen.

Guidance

Father, I come to sit at Your feet for guidance. May You lead me today with direction. I pray that You provide me with clarity and wisdom into Your truth. God, order my steps by Your Holy Spirit. Let Your Word guide my choices. Being in control often helps me feel comfortable, but I have learned that my ways are not always what is best for me. You know better than I do and want the best for me. If my situation could be better, I know You are still working. I pray that You help me be patient and provide the light to my path now. Give me clarity when in need, and lead my way. I pray this in Jesus' name, Amen.

Healing/Sickness

Dear Father, I'm coming to You today as Your child, asking for Your divine healing. There's so much I don't understand about life, but I know You are the same yesterday, today, and tomorrow. I ask that You forgive me of my sins, cleanse me of my unrighteousness, and begin Your healing from the inside out. I offer You no promises, bargains, or deals in exchange for my health. Instead, I bow my heart before You, believing You have the power to heal. If You use doctors to provide healing, give them the wisdom to know what to do and give me the direction of where to go. Regardless of how You accomplish it, the healing You give is always miraculous, and You deserve all the praise. In Jesus' name, Amen.

Heaven

Father, I thank You that because of who we are in Christ Jesus, we do not have to be filled with despair and worry over the things happening in the world today. You said we would have trials and tribulations while we are here, but to be of good cheer for You have overcome the world. You have equipped us with everything we need, and I thank You. When it's time to go home, You have prepared a place just for me. You said, "In My Father's house are many mansions. If it were not so, I would have told you. I go to prepare a place for you." You have promised never to abandon us like orphans and to return for us. Thank You for wanting humans to be a part of Your family since the beginning and for making a way. I love You and give You thanks and praise. In Jesus' name, Amen.

Holiness

Father, thank You for Your Word. Thank You for Your Holy Spirit. Thank You for showing me areas of my life that I need to repent of and change. You are set apart and blameless in every way. We will always benefit from Your decisions because of Your holiness and goodness. I pray You will continue to refine and shape me into the person You created me to be. I pray that You help me to pursue holiness in my life so that I can walk in obedience to Your Word and honor You. May my life testify to Your work in and through me. In Jesus' name, Amen.

Hope

Father God, Sometimes this world is hard to understand, and even when we trust You, our hearts still ache. So we come to You today asking for the hope that sees past the here and now to the then and there. Hope that holds our hearts up in the moments when life brings us to our knees. You are the only one who can sustain us. You are the only one who can save us. Be the rescuer of our souls, the deliverer of our dreams, the holder of our hearts. We believe that even the darkest night must lead to dawn. We wait with expectation. Give us courage. Surround us with comfort. Love us through to the other side in the way only You can. We put our hope, and our hopes for those we love, in You. We do this in the mighty name of Jesus, Amen.

Identity

Father, help me remember that I am part of a chosen generation. We are a royal priesthood, a holy nation, and one of Your special people. You created humankind in Your image, and You make no mistakes. Which means we are perfect just the way we are. Thank You for making us beautiful. When we look in a mirror, help us to see ourselves exactly as You see us. Give us a new and fresh perspective on who we are in Your eyes. Let us see others through Your eyes as well. In Jesus' name, Amen.

Joy

Father, I need Your help to find joy again. My body and mind are tired and weak from searching for inner peace and reasons to rejoice. I pray for physical and mental strength to find the joy that will make my smile shine and keep my spirit from growing weary. I need You near me each moment so that joy can consume my spirit. Without You, there is no contentment with life and no pleasure to light up my soul. Be with me now and help me to find joy in my surroundings and circumstances. In Jesus' name, I pray, Amen.

Life

Dear Father, thank You for another day. Thank You for waking me up and giving me the breath in my lungs. Thank You for the friends and family that are in my life. Thank You for allowing us to be Your hands and feet every day. As the sun rises, may Your love increase in my heart. A love that builds relationships develops trust and demonstrates a love that can only come from You. Please help me not to waste this day. My time here on earth has meaning because the people here are important. Lord, may I live in the light of Your love, and may You receive all the praise. In Jesus' name, Amen.

Lonely

Heavenly Father, I need You. It feels like no one understands what I am going through. I feel alone and unseen. My heart aches, and I feel sadness. I am coming to You, dear Father, asking for Your comfort. I am praying for You to remind me that I am not alone. You see me. The most important relationship that I can have is one with You. Even if I feel like no one else sees or listens to me, I know You are with me. You are listening to my every thought and word. Hold me in Your loving arms. Fill me with Your presence and remind me that I am never alone. In Jesus' name, Amen.

Love

Father, I thank You that there is no human experience I might walk through where Your love cannot reach me. If I climb the highest mountain, You are there. If I find myself in the darkest valley of my life, You are there. Help me to rest in that love that asks nothing more than the simple trusting heart of a child. Father, help me to see others through Your eyes so that the love You have shown me, I can give to them. Thank You for Your love and all the people that You have placed in my life who have demonstrated Your love. What a blessing it is, and I give thanks and praise in Jesus' name, Amen.

Marriage

Dear Heavenly Father, help us to have You at the center of our marriage. Give us a fresh hunger for seeking Your truth- individually and as a couple. Father, direct our steps. In our relationship, may we always communicate with You and one another. Keep us in Your Word and in prayer. May our love for You and one another be reflected in our walk. Open our hearts to fully cherish each other and open our eyes to see the blessings we have. May we never take these vows for granted but fulfill them with honor and strength. It is in Jesus' name we pray, Amen.

Meditation

Father, quiet my heart and mind as I wait on You. I want to focus on You, Father, and shut out all the world's distractions. Right now, it is just You and me, Father. As I think about the truths in Your Word, may the meditation of my heart be sweet and honoring to You. Empty me of self as the Holy Spirit fills me with Your love and truth. I need You and love You, Lord. I ask that You speak to me through Your Word in these quiet moments together. I'm listening and anticipating as I read and meditate on Your beautiful Word. In Jesus' name, Amen.

Mercy

Father, I have sinned against You and confess my sins before You. My heart desires to turn away from all my sins and back to You. Thank You that Your mercy towards me never fails. Thank You that Your loving-kindness towards all Your children and I are new every morning. Thank You for remaining faithful to the promises You have made to me. That whosoever believes in Jesus will not perish but have everlasting life. Thank You that Christ's death on the cross has washed away all my past, present, and future sins. Lord, from this day forward, help me to learn to take every thought captive and give it to You, and wash my heart clean and pure so that I live and work to Your honor and glory. In Jesus' precious name, I pray, Amen.

Obedience

Dear Father, I humbly call upon You for help to live a life that is pleasing to You. Thank You for the rich deposit of the Holy Spirit that draws us close to You. He is the one who brings conviction to our hearts when we sin against You and others. Help me, Father, to be obedient to Your voice as I read Your Word and seek in my heart all that You call me to be and do! I confess and ask for forgiveness for wanting my way over obedience to Your voice. Father, help me to desire Your will and not the desire of the flesh. Thank You for Your grace and mercy through this journey. Thank You for wanting me to be a part of Your family. Be with me now as I turn from my sin and go forth being obedient to Your Word. In Jesus' name, Amen.

Patience

Father, I pray that You will help me recognize when my emotions are building up into frustration or when I am starting to become irritated inside. Help me to hand over these feelings to You immediately. Enable me to grow in grace and to develop a patient spirit and humility of heart. Help me to live out the new identity that You have granted me through Your Son, Christ Jesus. Forgive me for being impatient with others. Help me now to demonstrate patience and love in my walk. I want my walk in this life to point people back to You, a loving Father. Be with me now, O God. Fill me with patience, and may You receive all the glory. In Jesus' name, Amen.

Peace

Father, I come before You ready to pour out my worries, anxieties, and fears at Your feet. Bring peace into my soul that passes all worldly understanding and make me a light for others to see Your strength. I can't control people, plans, or all my circumstances, but I can yield those things to You and focus on Your goodness. Thank You today for every good gift You've given, every blessing You've sent, all the forgiveness I did not deserve, and, yes, for every trial You've allowed into my life. You bring good out of every circumstance if I only let go and believe You. Help me to let go and trust in You, Lord. In Jesus' name, Amen.

Praise

Thank You, Father, for the opportunity of worship. Thank You that in prayer, we can put aside the uncertainties of this world and rest upon the certainties of the Kingdom. Thank You that Your promises are not changeable. Thank You that Your strength and assurance are all that we require. Blessed are You, Lord God. Great is Your mercy for Your people. Cleanse our hearts and lives with Your Holy Word; may our prayers please You. Help us to let our light shine before others and lead them to the way of faith. I come to You now full of thanks and praise in Jesus' name, Amen.

Prayer

Father, as I come to You with my heart leading the way, I ask that You strengthen my prayer life. I know a relationship can only grow with communication. I pray You will help us all to see how important it is to come to You. We make time for many things in this world, yet You are the most important. Father, thank You that I can turn to You. Thank You for Your love and desire to hear from me. Help those who may struggle and not know what to pray. Help them to see that it is just a conversation and that You love them and want to hear from them. Thank You for all that You have done and have yet to do. In Jesus' name, Amen.

Protection

Dear Father, thank You for another day. Thank You for my friends and family. I come before You now, asking that You surround us with Your angels to watch over us and protect us as we go through this day. Protect not only our bodies but our minds. Help us to be still and trust in You. Help us to renew our minds to You as we begin another day. Thank You for Your word. I know that You are faithful and will strengthen us and protect us from the evil one. Be with me now, Father; be with my friends and family. Guide us through this day and protect us along the way. In Jesus' name, I pray, Amen.

Purpose

Father God, I acknowledge that my life is not my own. I am Your handiwork, created in Christ Jesus to do good works. I live to bring glory to Your name. I pray that You reveal my purpose in Your Kingdom. Please help me to see my assignment for this season. I want to be used by You, oh God. I pray that You remove the people and habits from my life that block Your purpose in me. I lay my will aside and submit to Your plans for my life. Thank You, Father, for choosing me. Thank You for the Holy Spirit that guides me. Be with me now, and may every step I take be in the direction that serves You. In Jesus' name, I pray, Amen.

Rebellions

Gracious Father, You are sovereign and holy, compassionate and faithful. You created us to be in a loving relationship with You. You seek to shape us and guide us by Your perfect will. Yet, we rebel against Your will and seek our way. We choose to follow our desires, even when they are destructive. Our hearts are rebellious as we do what we think is right. You have called us to deny ourselves, take up our cross, and follow You. Forgive us for missing the mark. Forgive us for slipping away. Forgive us for our sinful nature and actions. Transform our lives with the power of Your Spirit. Redeem and restore us to glorify You. In Jesus' name, Amen.

Redemption

Father, thank You that for our redemption, You gave Your only-begotten Son to the death of the cross, and His glorious resurrection delivered us from the power of our enemy. Thank You that we who trust in Jesus Christ as our Lord and Saviour have redemption through His blood. May we never forget the price paid for our sins. Help us each day to live this life You have blessed us with, to give honor and praise to You. In Jesus' name, Amen.

Repentance

Father, today I'm confessing my desperate need for You. You have promised that if we confess our sins, You will forgive us and make us clean again. So I want to turn from my ways and come to You. Father, as I ask for forgiveness, I also forgive those who have done wrong against me. I am no better than anyone else, and I thank You for teaching me this through demonstrating Your love and grace. Thank You for having a plan to save a dying world. Thank You for wanting us as family and trusting in us to be a light in the world that reflects Your grace and love to others. In Jesus' name, Amen.

Rest

Our loving Father, we know You desire good things for Your children. Through our difficulties and troubles, we know that You are fighting for our good. We can rest securely in Your arms, knowing that Your victory is sure and that You go with us along our way. Teach our minds to rest in Your truth. Teach our hearts to rest in Your love and our bodies to rest in Your peace. As we rest in You, we ask that You fill us with Your joy and peace. We love You, and we thank You for the love that You have for us. In Jesus' name, we pray, Amen.

Righteousness

Father God, I cannot do righteousness; I can only receive it. I pray for divine strength and spiritual endurance right now. I lack nothing, including righteousness, when I surrender my life to You. I ask that You now guard my heart and emotions with the breastplate of righteousness. Root out any sin hindering my journey in pursuing Your righteousness. Thank You for always being with me. Thank You for the robe of righteousness given to me through Your son Jesus Christ and for the Holy Spirit, which You use to draw me closer to You. May my hunger and thirst for righteousness never grow dull or be quenched. In Jesus' name, I pray, Amen.

Salvation

Heavenly Father, I believe You sent Your only begotten Son, Jesus Christ, to die on the cross so that I am forgiven of my sins by believing in Him. I confess, Lord, that I am a sinner and need a Saviour. I believe that Jesus Christ died on the cross to pay the price for my sins, for He alone lived a sinless life and died as an innocent man.

Father, I repent of all my sins and turn away from them. I pray that You would keep me holy and set apart for You. Moving forward, I seek to live my life for You. Guide my path now. In Jesus' name, I pray, Amen.

Satan

Father, I can sometimes recognize when my enemy is at work again. He tries to discourage me, get me sidetracked, have me fall into temptation, and take my eyes off You. He's always at work. Thank You for the power of the Holy Spirit that fills me with wisdom and discernment to make me aware of the enemy's traps so I can stand firm against his schemes. Your Word teaches me that He who is in me is greater than he who is in the world. Thank You, Father, for the blood of Jesus that washes away my sins and for the Holy Spirit that guides me. In Jesus' name, Amen.

Scripture

Father, through the prophet Isaiah's words, we are reminded that Your Word does not return void but accomplishes what You desire. It is a lamp unto our feet and a light for our path. Your Word is divinely inspired and useful for teaching, rebuking, correcting, and training in righteousness, so we are thoroughly equipped for every good work. Thank You, Father, for Your Word. We are grateful for the guidance we receive through faithfully reading and applying scripture to our lives. It is in Jesus' name that we come before You now in prayer and with thanks, Amen.

Security

Father, evil is such a harsh word, yet Your Word uses it frequently to describe the opposite of good. While we are all capable of sin, I ask that You protect us from those who scheme against righteousness and twist the truth into lies to accomplish their evil intents. Surround us with Your angels to protect us from dark, spiritual forces we cannot see.

You will bring justice for all the harm and needless violence aimed at Your children in due time. Until then, we will be in Your presence, aligned with Your purposes, and we look to You as our Supreme Commander and Protector. Help us to avoid temptation and deliver us from evil, Lord. In Jesus' name, Amen.

Self-Worth

Heavenly Father, I come to You today with a humble heart and a desire for self-worth. Remind me again where my worth comes from. I pray that You will help me see myself as the beautiful creation You created. I pray that You will allow me to see that my imperfections are not flaws but simply part of the design that makes me unique. I pray that You will help me see that the things I have done wrong in life do not define who I am now or who I will become. As Your child, help me now to know my worth. I am created in Your image to be a light in this world. Thank You, Father, in Jesus' name, Amen.

Serving

O, Heavenly Father, give me a heart like the heart of Jesus, ready to serve than be served. May Your life of love and service guide me to loving and serving others. I pray to see the needs of others around me and respond with compassion and love. Help me see the gifts and talents You have blessed me with and use them to serve others. Thank You for having a plan for me. Thank You for Your love and grace. Help me now to demonstrate the same passion as I go through this day. And may You receive all the glory, in Jesus' name I pray, Amen.

Singleness

Father, I ask that You look down with grace and mercy on all single men and women who desire to be married yet remain single. I pray that You look with compassion on the desires of their hearts. Bring a person of Your choosing into their life, with whom they can share their life and future. I pray that during the time of waiting, You would guard their hearts and minds with the assurance that You know the intimate desires and needs of their hearts and that in Your time and in Your way, You will bring into their life the person that You have been preparing for them. Pour into each heart a stillness and peace that comes only from You. I ask this in Jesus' name, Amen.

Stability

Dear Lord, please tune my ear to Your voice today. I want to be sensitive to Your Spirit. Quiet the noise of the world, the flesh, and the enemy. Soothe my soul with Your still, small voice. Allow me to hear Your Words above the relentless roars of the enemy. Silence my inner critic and help me to stay firmly planted on the solid ground of the truth. Thank You for giving me the stability of knowing You and allowing me to rest in You as my source of strength, peace, and stability. Guide my steps now, in Jesus' name, Amen.

Stewardship

Generous and loving Father, we offer You thanks and praise as we recognize that all we receive comes from You. Guide us now as stewards of Your abundance and caretakers of all You have entrusted us. Father, help us be faithful stewards of our time, talents, and wealth. May the Holy Spirit open our hearts to see the needs of others so that we may share all that You have blessed us with in a loving way that gives glory to You. In Jesus' name, Amen.

Strength

Father, I am so tired of trying to weather the storms of life on my own. I need Your power and strength to face each one. Please give me the strength to endure this season of life that is weighing me down. Help me during these challenging times, and may I honor You in the midst of them as I walk by faith. I believe Your Word in Isaiah 41:10. You are with me; You will strengthen and help me. You will uphold me by Your righteous right hand. Nothing in this world can separate me from Your steadfast love. I give You thanks and praise, in Jesus' name, Amen.

Temptation

Oh Father, I ask for Your strength and help to resist temptations and not to give in. Help me to take every tempting thought captive and hand it over to You before it takes hold of me. Help me in my weakness to know You as my strength, and help me in my foolishness to know You as my wisdom. For the sins I have committed, I ask that You forgive me now, as I forgive those who have sinned against me. Thank You for Your grace and mercy, Lord. Thank You for providing a way out so we may endure sin. Thank You for the blood of Jesus that washes away our sins and for the authority that You have given us so that we do not have to be a slave to sin. I love You and thank You in Jesus' name, Amen.

Thankfulness

Father, how I praise You, Lord, for each day of my life. For my family, friends, and all the good things You have provided me in Your love and grace. Thank You that Jesus Christ's blood spilled on the cross has washed away all my sins, cleansed, and made me whole. Thank You that Jesus rose again on the third day and ascended on high, bringing eternal life and conquering death. Thank You for sending the Holy Spirit to be my helper. I pray that I live my life in a manner that glorifies You. I ask that You use my life to share the gospel. I give you all thanks and glory. In Jesus' name, Amen.

Thoughts

Father, You gave me Your Word as a weapon to fight impure and unholy thoughts. Thank You for giving me authority over every plan that the enemy may have. Thank You for the Holy Spirit that lives within me and guides my ways. You know all of my thoughts and the attitudes of my heart. May my spoken words and unspoken thoughts be pleasing in Your sight, O Lord, my rock and my redeemer. The enemy is ready to battle and never rest. Be with me now this day, Lord. Give me the helmet of salvation to guard my mind and heart against unhealthy thoughts. In Jesus' name, I pray, Amen.

Trouble

Father God, help me to trust in You with all my heart and not lean on my understanding, but in all my ways submit to You. I know there will be times of suffering and hardship in this life, but help me take heart knowing that You have overcome the world. Please give me the courage to face the challenges that come my way and help me to persevere and not give up. May You be my strength. Pour out Your love over me and keep me in Your perfect peace. Thank You, Lord Jesus, for Your help through this challenging season. I know You've got this, and You've got me! I praise You and put all my faith and trust in You. Father, thank You for this time and for being able to come to You in prayer. In Jesus' name, Amen.

Trust

Jesus, my Savior, came to earth to save me and told me to believe in You. My mind knows that if I trust and have faith in You, You will be with me. Erase my doubt, Father. Take it all away. Help my unbelief. You are the great "I AM." You are faithful to Your promises and have given me authority over the enemy. I will not be discouraged because I walk in Your divine presence. I will live in Your strength and courage, for You are my God. I have faith in You and Your Word because I know that Your Word never fails. I thank You for the many promises You have spoken over my life, and I trust You. In Jesus' name, Amen.

Truth

Father God, today we put on the whole armor of God to guard our lives against attack. We give particular importance to putting on the belt of truth to protect us against the enemy's lies and deception. You promised that Your Holy Spirit would guide Your children into all truth, especially those who seek You wholeheartedly.

Keep me, I pray, and show me in my life as I read Your Word and study the scriptures. Prevent me, Lord, from being swept into the many false doctrines. Give me a discerning heart, I pray, and help me find a teacher to teach me the whole council of Your Word of Truth so that I may grow in grace and knowledge of the Lord Jesus Christ. In Jesus' name, I pray, Amen.

Unsaved

Father, Your Word commands us to go into the world so that the lost may receive the forgiveness of their sins and an inheritance among those sanctified by faith in You! Use me to reach my family, neighbors, city, and beyond so that You alone will receive the glory! Thank You for the greatest act of sacrificial love – dying on the cross for my salvation and the salvation of all those who have yet to call You Lord and Savior. Father, in John 17:3, Jesus was praying that people come to know You, our only means to eternal salvation. Today, I pray as Jesus did and ask that You help those who have yet to give their lives to Christ. May Your love and power reveal themselves to the nonbelievers so they will someday know You. In Jesus' name, Amen.

Victory

Dear Father, We know that we wrestle not against flesh and blood but against spiritual rulers and forces of evil. Please help me to gird up my mind with the gospel of truth and to buckle on the breastplate of righteousness as I walk in the way of peace. Help me maintain my trust in You and protect my heart and mind with my salvation in Christ. Equip me, I pray, with the sword of the spirit, which is the Word of God, so that I may be able to protect myself against the deceptive teachings and doctrines of demons that lead so many astray. I give thanks to our Lord Jesus Christ, knowing that it is in Him alone that our victory rests. Thank You for being with me and fighting my enemies. In Jesus' name, Amen.

Wisdom

Father God, I ask for Your guidance as I go about my day. I ask in faith that as Your Word promises me, You will give me wisdom in every small and large decision as I step into my purpose today. I don't want the shallow knowledge this world pretends to provide, nor do I want to rely on my understanding. I desire your wisdom in my life. Thank you for being patient, forgiving, and loving enough to hear my prayer. Thank You for the Holy Spirit that teaches and guides me in Your truth. Be with me now, in Jesus' name, Amen.

Witnessing

Father, I have family, friends, and neighbors who do not seem to know You. It troubles me that they do not know You, the true God. They struggle like I do but only have their strength to get through each day. I don't want them to miss out on the resurrection of life and the glorious new heavens and earth. Therefore, I ask You to strengthen me to be a faithful witness. Give me the words needed to provide them an opportunity to know You as their Lord and Savior. Prepare their heart to listen and receive Your message, the message that gives life to all who receive it. Please help me to be loving, bold, and wise.

I look forward to seeing You do amazing things throughout my life and to You being all the glory! In the precious name of Jesus', I pray, Amen.

Work

Heavenly Father, what a glorious future You have purposed and planned for all who trust Christ as their Lord and Saviour. May I never doubt Your Word, but enable me to be steadfast in my daily walk and strong in my Christian faith. Help me to be productive during my time on earth and allow me to carry out Your work and Your will, knowing that my toil is not fruitless in Christ. Thank You for the truth of the Resurrection and the knowledge that this mortal body will put on immortality at Your appointed time. Help me remain occupied in the work that You have prepared for me. You get all the praise and glory in Jesus' name, Amen.

Worried

Father, it is so easy to be a worrier. We live in a day where there is much to worry about, be concerned about, and be anxious over. You have told us not to be anxious about anything, but in every situation, by prayer and petition, with thanksgiving, to present our requests to God. Father, I need You to help me move from worry to worship. Rather than be anxious, I want to look up to the heavens and talk with You. Please give me the grace and the ability to make this transition. Father, remind me that the one in control of everything is You. You hold the whole world in Your hands, including me. Thank You for loving me, caring for me, and being with me every day. In Jesus' name, Amen.

About the author

 **Keith Gwaltney** was raised in Jacksonville, Florida, and worked 25 years as a Correctional Officer and two years as a bailiff before retiring in Fleming Island, Florida.

From a young age, Keith was always interested in magic tricks and being creative. Since 2004, he has performed at kids' parties, corporate events, and on stages. Growing up as a shy kid, he often wondered how he was able to perform in front of large crowds.

In 2014, God laid it on Keith's heart to share the gospel with the talent that he has been given. It took Keith three years to embrace what God had shown him and to realize this is why he could stand before an audience and speak.

More about the author

Today, Keith creates messages for schools, churches, and his YouTube channel. The first unique magic trick he created, "Sharing Jesus," is for sale on one of the largest magic sites on the internet. He has incorporated sharing the gospel by making the Visual Ministries platform. Through Visual Ministries, he has a program called S.H.I.N.E. (Sharing His Image Now to Everyone) and is publishing his second book "Prayers for Everyday Living."

As far as the future goes, Keith wants to continue growing in his relationship with God and as well as to share His Word and love through magic, books, and everyday actions. You can follow or contact Keith Gwaltney at:

Website: kgmagic.com

YouTube: https://www.youtube.com/@KeithGwaltney

Available through Amazon

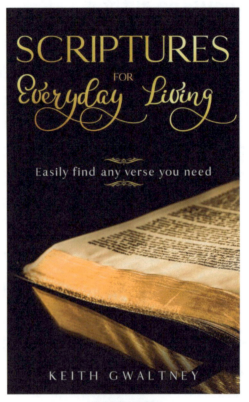

ORDER HERE

Made in the USA
Columbia, SC
28 December 2023